Take the Risks

or

Get a Job

How to Make the Choices That Will Make You More Money!

Michele A. Scism

Thanks Christie,
Be Decisive
Michele A Scism

Michele A. Scism
4845 Lake Street PMB 125
Lake Charles, LA 70605
Info@DecisiveMinds.com
www.DecisiveMinds.com

ISBN 978-0-9826816-5-7

First edition March 2014

Limits of Liability and Disclaimer of Warranty

The author and publisher shall not be liable for your misuse of this material. This book is strictly for informational and educational purposes.

Warning – Disclaimer

The purpose of this book is to educate and entertain. The author and/or publisher do not guarantee that anyone following these techniques, suggestions, tips, ideas, or strategies will become successful. The author and/or publisher shall have neither liability nor responsibility to anyone with respect to any loss or damage caused, or alleged to be caused, directly or indirectly by the information contained in this book.

Book cover designed by Jena Rodriguez, AROD Web Design

I dedicate this book to the men and women who live their lives courageously as entrepreneurs. It takes courage, dedication, strength and decisiveness.

A special thank you to my parents, Johnny and Clo Mere for being my entrepreneurial role models!

And to Suzanne Evans and Larry Winget for kicking me in the butt to get this book done.

Get your **FREE** Companion Video Series
"From Under Earning Expert to Highly Paid Authority"
at

www.HighlyPaidAuthority.com

You will also receive weekly business tips designed specifically for decisive business owners.

You will learn.......

- How to use VIP days to work with clients, add money to your bottom line and have diversity in your offerings.
- How to turn your $10 book or e-book into a $200 product.
- How to increase your conversions and double your sales this year.

If you are ready to start making more money in your business be sure to a quick look at these 3 short videos that are packed with information that you can apply immediately.

So let's get started!

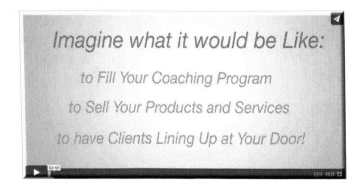

www.HighlyPaid Authority.com

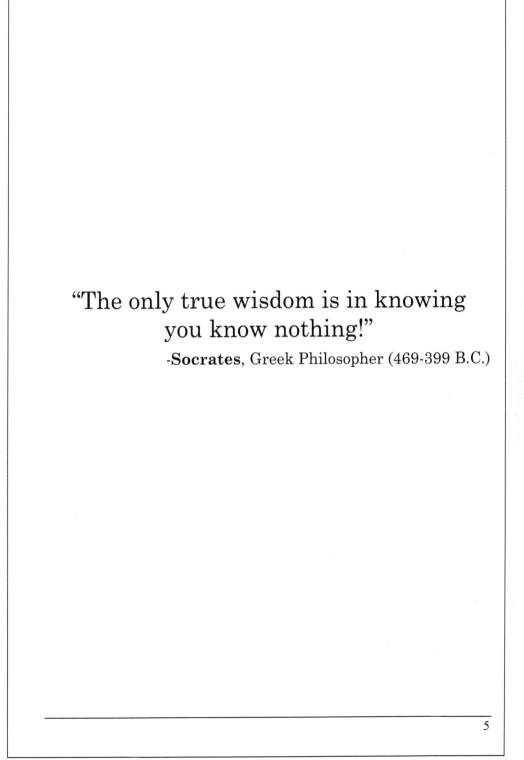

"The only true wisdom is in knowing
you know nothing!"

-**Socrates**, Greek Philosopher (469-399 B.C.)

Contents

Preface

Entrepreneurs are facing an epidemic. "Business Failure" seems to be the phrase of the day and most entrepreneurs seem to have one fact in common…. They are broke!

The good news is that this is completely self made and as such is fixable. The bad news is that this is completely self made and as such is hard to fix because what you have done to get here isn't going to be what it takes to fix it. What is required is that you become a courageous business owner who is empowered to take calculated risks that will bring great return on investment.

If you are looking for that get rich quick with a 4 hour work week b.s. you're in the wrong place. And please don't tell me you think your circumstances have created the problem. Ok I get it – your family and friends don't understand and your employees seem to lack commitment. Welcome to entrepreneurship. If you are resigned to blame your circumstances then you might have a problem with this book.

Are you a small business owner or an entrepreneur who has cash flow but who just never seems to have any money? When you need money it always seems to work out but there are many times when you worry about how you are going to cover your bills. You might have even bought into the lies that all you need is passion, a dream and a desire to have a successful business. How is that working for you?

Oh and I'll just say it – this book is not for lazy, whinny or complacent entrepreneurs. If you are ok with the struggle, resigned to the fact that it must be hard and you are not ready to do what it takes to make money in your business then you can stop here. I wouldn't want to disappoint you.

You see I have a desire to see you make more money than you can even imagine at this moment. Imagine if you could build your business to a point where it was making so much money that someone actually wanted to buy it from you.

I know exactly what that is like but I also know what it's like when you can't pay your bills. You know those moments when you mail the check without the signature on purpose.

In 1990 the phone rang in our office and it was the banker. He was calling to say the bank no longer believed our family business was a "viable" business and they wanted their $1.5 Million back. After begging the bank not to take everything we owned we knew we had to change the way we did business. We realized we had to start competing on quality instead of price, we had to learn more about our ideal clients than they knew about themselves and we had to go through our financials with a fine tooth comb. 17 years later we got another phone call. This time it was someone wanting to buy our company. The sale price ended up being $9 Million.

Entrepreneurship isn't for everyone. It isn't easy. It requires guts, risks, courage and sometimes blind faith. Are you ready? How bad do you want it?

"The key to success is
to be the last one standing!"

-Suzanne Evans,
Author of *"The Way You Do Anything
is the Way You Do Everything"*

How's That Working For You?

It was a hot, muggy summer day in Louisiana in 1990 when my phone rang. My gut wrenched when I heard the voice say "Hey Michele, it's Gary." You see Gary was our banker and he was calling to say he was on his way over and he wanted to make sure we were at the office and ready to talk. We knew it wasn't going to be a pleasant conversation because our 15 year old family trucking business was in trouble.

Gary had a message for us from his boss. The bank no longer thought that our company was a "viable" business and they wanted to close our $1.5 Million dollar line of credit. And if you haven't been in that position before that means they want their money back. What would you do in that moment? Would you give up and start selling everything you had or would you become creative? Would your entrepreneurial instincts kick in?

I have to say this was probably the turning point in the way I looked at entrepreneurship. I had grown up as an entrepreneur in a family of entrepreneurs and what I watched my dad do in this instance changed the way I approach everything in life.

First he reminded the bank that at that point we had been a customer of theirs for over 50 years with our other businesses and that there had been a couple of times during those 50 years when certain businesses got in trouble. Every single time we were able to pull the business out or revamp it in a way that we were able to pay back all the money.

Then he asked for a little time to figure this out. We knew that there were things that we were going to have to change in the business to increase the cash flow to be able to fix the problem. In the meantime, my dad visited the bank to find out about any federal programs that might have been able to help us. I don't know if you remember but in the 1980's and 1990's there were a lot of bank defaults happening in the United States and around the world.

The bank actually found a federal program that was designed to help failing companies pay back their principal without having to pay interest. You see in the 1980's interest rates on these types of loans were hovering in the low 20% range. They were ridiculously high and had started to come down in the late 1980's and early 1990's but so many businesses were defaulting because their interest rates were so high.

The agreement with the bank was a 0% interest loan that was being backed by the federal government for 3 years. That gave us the ability to pay down our loan, not pay it off but drastically pay it down. At the same time we were able to revamp our business, restructure our equipment, focus more closely on what our clients desired and improve collections.

Long story short, in 2005 we received another phone call. It was someone wanting to know if our trucking business was for sale. At first we said "No!" but then we started to look at it as a possibility. We did not close the deal with the first guy or the second guy but in 2007 we did close a deal for $9 Million with a great company and my entire family retired from the trucking industry.

"Just ask! You may be shocked what they will give you." ~Johnny Mere

What's your wakeup call?

Have you had that defining moment when you faced the fear of losing it all? Maybe it is simply that you don't have enough clients to keep the cash flowing, maybe it is that you haven't been picking up the phone to follow up with potential clients or maybe you don't have a clue what it is but you know you're in trouble.

What I hope you take away from that story is that you have to have the guts to go after what you not only want but need and the second is that even when it looks the darkest, and trust me it was dark, it is possible to pull it out when you don't curl up and give up. You see we could have hidden from the problem and actually that was what got us there in the first place. We were not facing the problem head on pro actively.

Are you seriously ready to make a change?

Not just I think I'm ready. You have to be so ready that you are willing to do whatever it takes. I recently read a great book by one of my mentors, Suzanne Evans, called "*The Way You Do Anything is the Way You Do Everything*." In that book she said "Your profits mirror your choices. Your successes mirror your commitments. Your cash flow is a reflection of the consistency of everything in your life." Think about that. What choices are you making in business on a daily basis? Did you choose to make the follow up call or did you choose to clean out the desk drawer? Can you truly say you are 100% committed to your business? Don't just blow this off, what is your commitment level? Are you willing to go without sleep? Are you willing to stand up in front of everyone and be loud and proud about the solutions to provide to their problems?

You know for me that was a tough one. I am an extremely shy introvert. I will tell you the story about me starting Decisive Minds a little later in this book but that first year in this business was awful. I made a whole $12,000 in that year and I made all of that in the last 6 months of the year. You see I had two problems from the beginning – SHY and INTROVERTED! So when I started this business I said "I am not speaking or networking!"

Thank God I had hired a business coach before I started this business. He never let up. He prodded, pocked and insisted I start speaking to let people know who I was and what I could do. He was right. Now it did take me the full twelve months to actually give my first in person talk but at six months I started teaching teleseminars on the phone. I figured if I could hide behind the phone I would be alright.

It was one of the scariest things I had to do but it changed the course of my business. From those humble beginnings in 2010 and then in September of 2013 I stood on a stage in Houston, TX and sold $300,000 in coaching programs. How committed are you?

REMEMBER........

Today's Results = Your Activities 90 Days Ago

R.O.I.

www.DecisiveMinds.com

"The truth will set you free
but first it will piss you off!"

-Gloria Steinem,
Feminist, Journalist, Social Activist

The Truth is...You're Broke

In 2011 my then 17 year old son walked into my home office and said "Mom you are the Lebron James of business women." For those of you who have sons, I dare say that is by far the best compliment you can get from a 17 year old boy. Now if you have multiple children then you would probably agree that they don't like to be shown up by their siblings. Not to be out done, a few days later my then 20 year old daughter walked into my office and said "Mom you are the white Oprah." Now I don't know if that's because I help so many people or because I hand her so much money but it did get me thinking. Many things went through my head and one of them was what it would be like to have "Oprah Kind of Money".

Do you ever dream about what it would be like to have Oprah kind of money? We actually talk about it all the time at my house. Think of all the great things you could do if you had that kind of money?

I would start by funding Alzheimer's research facilities. My 92 year old grandmother died recently from Alzheimer's. It is a terrible disease.

I would also fund co-working spaces around the country so small business owners would have affordable office space while they are building their businesses. My big dream is to help 1000 entrepreneurs build Million dollar businesses.

Oh and don't think I wouldn't splurge. I don't know if you know but I like to travel in style. 5 star all the way baby. So I would buy a new RV. Not just any RV but top of the line which of course at this moment in time is a *Provost* and I know exactly which one I want. It's called *The Elegant Lady*.

How perfect is that? Of course it would have a driver. I've had lots of offers for that position already.

And I would no longer have just one *Coach* Purse I would have a closet full of *Coach* Purses.

Oh and I would have my own reality show like Marcus Lemonis' show *"The Profit"*. It's one of my all time favorite shows where he goes into failing businesses and invests his own money and time to help them fix their business. Doesn't that sound amazing? Did you think of some things you could do if you had "Oprah Kind of Money"?

Now my guess is that you are sitting there thinking that this all sounds great but that it is not your reality. And you're right. I know you don't necessarily need proof but check this out.

*****

Did you know that according to Reuters' the average 50 year old has $2500 in the bank?

*****

According to The Huffington Post, if you make more than $100K a year, you make more than 92.6% of Americans.

*****

According to CNN Money, Americans are $7.7 Trillion poorer than they were in 2007.

*****

The fact is: People are broke!

And we all know that big business is broke. Whatever happened to the Sharper Image or Circuit City? They are gone. The good news is that at this moment in time Sears is "still open" but barely.

Oh and I don't know if you heard but the United States Government is also broke. Don't worry – it's only $77 trillion in debt.

And entrepreneurs are broke. You are broke. I know how it is. You sit at your desk and wonder why this is so hard. Oh you might even be saying "Michele, I'm not broke. I pay my bills." Don't kid yourself. Yea, you have money coming in but you are still struggling. You don't have as much money as you want and you don't have as much as you deserve. You know what. There was a time in my life when we were doing $15 Million in annual sales in the trucking company and I was broke. Just because you have cash flow doesn't mean you aren't broke. How much of that money are you keeping? Is it taking every dime to keep your business going?

You know when my kids walked into my office and said those amazing things I thought "Well if that is true then why am I still so broke? Why is this so hard?" Are you feeling that?

The question is "How bad do you want it?"

There is a great Greek Fable about Socrates. One day a young man walked up to Socrates and asked him how to be successful. Socrates told the young man to meet him at the beach the following morning. At the beach Socrates took the young man by the hand and led him out into the water. When they were about chest deep Socrates grabbed the young man's head and pushed him under the water. The young man fought for a moment and Socrates pulled him up and asked "Young man, what do you want?" "To know how to be successful" the young man answered so Socrates pushed him under the water again.

This time the young man fought a little harder and Socrates pulled him up again asking "Young man, what do you want?" "To be rich" the young man answered. This time Socrates pushed him under and held him under till the very moment before the young man thought he might pass out. When he pulled him up he asked again "Young man, what do you want" "To breath" the young man answered. Socrates said **"When you want success as much as you want to breathe then and only then will you find it."**

So again, I ask you **"How Bad Do You Want It?"**

Even the successful ones are broke

How many times do you look at the leaders in your industry and think "Someday I am going to have a business just like theirs." From the outside it looks like they have it all. They have lots of clients, they are always traveling, wearing the best suits, carrying the newest *Coach* Purse but the reality is that they are barely making it. They are up late at night trying to figure out how they are going to get enough money this week to cover payroll. The fact is that it doesn't matter what level your business is if you are making poor choices, you stay broke.

Broke is a Choice

OK, I know you're thinking "Did she just say that? Did she just say I am choosing to be broke?" Yes, she did because it's true. Your poor choices are keeping you broke.

One of my clients, Belanie Dishong (LiveAtChoice.com), teaches people how to have amazing relationships whether that is with other people, your career or your money. One of the things she teaches is that we are 100% responsible for everything that shows up in our lives. We choose it based on our words. I have heard her talk often about imagining a shelf with everything on it. It has new clients next to no clients, it has "I'll always be broke" next to "I have abundant financial success", and it has "This is too hard" next to "Money flows easily". The trick is to choose wisely.

You must start paying close attention to what you say and what you think because that is what you are getting. The great news is that you have the ability to turn that around. Stop right now! Listen to what you are saying and thinking. Do this for a day, a week, a month and you will start to see the patterns and what I can promise you is that you are getting what you ask for.

I doubt this is a new theory for you. You have no doubt heard that all you have to do is ask for what you want, believe that you can have it and then be open to receive it. If you ever watched or read *"The Secret"* this is the theory that movie is based upon. The problem with that is that when it doesn't happen fast enough most people revert to their old ways. What is missing is the action.

After working with hundreds of entrepreneurs I can tell you that there are three things that stand between you and what you want. You're afraid, you're cheap and you're lazy. Each one of these has a direct connection to the missing actions that are keeping you broke.

Are you ready to do the work?

"You gain strength, courage and confidence by every experience by which you stop to look fear in the face. You must do the thing which you think you cannot do."

-Eleanor Roosevelt,
Former First Lady of the United States

Entrepreneurs Are Afraid

You cannot live in fear and be successful

You have to learn to **take a risk.** Listen we are all afraid of something but we can't let it control us if we want to accomplish our goals. I don't know about you but I am afraid of spiders but I don't move out of my house every time I see one. We all experience fear. It is our response to that fear that makes us stand out.

When we look at fear for the small business owner we pretty much hear the same ones all the time.

1. **The fear of SUCCESS!** Give me a break. This one I'm not going to let you get away with. If you didn't want success why did you start this business? Of course, you want success. Most people start businesses because they want more money, more control over their life, to spend more time with their family or they think their boss is an idiot and they can do it better than him. Achieving those would be success right? I don't think it is the fear of success. I think it is the fear of what the success will bring you. The fear of what it might take to grow your business.

2. **The fear of HIRING A TEAM!** Ask a successful entrepreneur what he did right and he will tell you that he surrounded himself with the best people he could find. I was in a meeting once with the president of a large organization and she said "When I sit in my board room with my team I want to feel like the dumbest person in the room. I want to know I have hired the smartest people I could." That takes courage. To not have to be the one who knows everything and does everything. What I have seen with my clients is that the fear around hiring a team is usually the concern of finding the right people, knowing how to train and manage them and what to pay them. What is worse than not attacking this fear head on is the reality of trying to build a business alone. It's not a business if you are the only employee. You have simply created a job for yourself. In my first book "Makeover Your Business in 6 Weeks or Less" I told the story of my father explaining that "you are only a business owner if you can leave your business, go on vacation and still make money while you are gone." I was very young when he taught me that but I got it. I have felt the pain of hiring the wrong people, not training people properly and having to re-do things but getting through the pain was worth it.

3. **The fear of SPENDING MORE MONEY!** It's true; you have to spend money to make money so it is understandable that you might be concerned that as your business grows you might have to spend more money. You might have to rent office space for all these employees. You would no longer be able to work in your third bedroom. And then there's furniture and computers and paper and ink. You might be expected to travel more and that's more money.

4. **The fear of SPENDING LESS TIME WITH YOUR FAMILY!** This is actually a fear I hear often. I know your family means everything to you. But have you stopped to really think about it? If you really had this business thing handled you could do some super cool things with your family. You could take them anywhere, you could show them anything, you could provide them with experiences you can't even imagine right now. Would there be times when you might not make it to dinner? Yes! Would there be times when things don't work out exactly as planned and you miss the baseball game? Yes! But as a third generation entrepreneur with two amazing children what I can tell you is that my way of life provided me the flexibility to do more with my children than most parents. You see you are worried that your business might keep you away but you have much more control over your time than those with a full time+ job. You can make the field trip because you have the flexibility.

5. **The fear of TAKING A RISK!** We finally made it to the big one. The one that is truly causing you the most pain. You're afraid of taking any action that will change your current situation. You're afraid to make it different than the way it is. Yet all of you say "I want it different than it is." It's the grand contradiction. The irony of it all is that you want it different but you don't want to do anything that makes it different. Because with that action comes the risk that both it might work and you would have to spend some money or more time or it might not work and you would be embarrassed.

Where to Start

For most entrepreneurs the first risk you need to take is a stand. You need a pick a direction. Get known for something. Chose a freaking topic and put it out there. Tell the world what you stand for. You know what; take your Kim Kardashian moment. She is definitely known for certain things, right? Taking a stand has made her rich. Don't get between Kim Kardashian and a camera, that girl knows the dollar value of being seen.

So listen, I get it. You are very talented. You can do 40 different things. Maybe you really want to be a copy writer but you know how to design websites and you can create beautiful e-book covers and if you don't tell people you do all those things then you might leave money on the table. The reality is though that people can't hire you because they have no clue what you do. You haven't taken a stand for any one thing so they are confused. Your website confuses them, your introduction confuses them and your offers confuse them.

I know this is scary. It's risky to choose a direction and put yourself out there as the authority in that area. You're probably even reading this trying every way in the world to argue with me when you know I'm right.

This is what really ticks me off. Your answer is sitting right in front of you. You know exactly what it is that you should be known for. The only thing wrong is that you are not committed to it. You're not willing to do whatever it takes to have the success in that particular industry. You want all the lights to be green before you can get in your car to take off. It doesn't work like that.

And I'm not just talking to the new entrepreneur. I know people who have been in business for years who still have not chosen a direction. About 6 months ago I was at an event and sitting with a woman who was doing over $200K in her business and she was saying to me "I just don't think I'm doing the right thing. I can't seem to grow. Maybe I should switch over to this topic." She was just starting to get the momentum and she was ready to bail.

Once you choose your direction you have to stick to it. No wishy washy I don't think its working stuff. If you have done the research, you understand what your consumers are looking for then it's time for you to take a stand and stick to it. For the first three years in this business I promoted myself as a social media coach. I would get people's attention by talking about social media and then when I had their attention I could talk to them about how to build their business.

Want to know the secret to choosing the correct direction? Choose something that your ideal clients, the people you really want to work with, are already looking for and spending money on. That's your easy in. When you do that like I did with social media they flock to you instead of you having to chase them.

So what is it that you are so afraid of?

What is it? Is it that you are afraid to take a stand because you might leave money on the table? We are all so eager to do anything and I completely understand that. When you don't have enough money it is really hard to think about missing out on any opportunities. But what I know to be true is that the more you say No to, the more you will have to say Yes to.

Or are you afraid to hire people because you might not be a good manager? You can't manage your own time how are you going to manage someone else's? Is it the fact that you might not be able to spend as much time with the kids or you might have to move out of that 3rd bedroom and rent space?

What does it take to get past this?

You have to feel the fear and do it anyway! There is a great book by Susan Jeffers with that title. Don't get me wrong, you're still going to be afraid. It just means that you don't let the fear stop you. How do you do that? You make a decision. You don't have to see the whole stair case just take the first step.

What's the best way to start – START!

How do you get over it – GET OVER IT!

Listen I am probably one of the most shy and introverted people you will ever meet. I face the fear every time I get on stage, or pick up the phone or meet my audience in the back of the room. But I don't let it stop me. I understand that by being the one standing on the stage and giving the talk I am being seen as a leading authority in business development. That makes it worth it to me. **What gets you through the fear is when what's on the other side of the fear is so important that it's worth it.** It's about that desire to get there.

Action Case Study #1

I remember when Lynn Ruby scheduled an appointment to talk to me for the 1st time. (RubyMarketingSystems.com) I thought "What is she calling me for? She looks like she has it all together." That was my perception but it wasn't her reality. She was a marketing coach in a sea of marketing coaches. She didn't have that thing she could take a stand for to get people's attention. Lynn is a brilliant marketer so it seemed too risky to get known for a single marketing aspect because there were so many things she could do for people. Do ever hear yourself say that? "But I could do this and I could do this oh but I can also do that" and you don't want to pick a single direction because you might miss a sale.

The secret is that when you lead with what people are already looking for they want to talk to you. When Lynn took the risk to say she was a video marketing coach, and thanks to YouTube everyone wants to know how to use video to market their business, people started to pay attention and she filled her coaching practice. Now along the way she had to take other risk. She had to consistently promote herself. She had to start speaking and being seen which meant spending money to sponsor events. What she realized is that what is on the other side is too important for her to let her fears stand in her way. Congratulations Lynn!

"Honesty is a very expensive gift.
Do not expect it from cheap people."

-Warren Buffett,
Business Magnet, Investor, Philanthropist

Entrepreneurs Are Cheap

We all know cheap!

You've got that aunt that shows up at every family reunion in her lime green stretch pants, you know the ones that glow in the dark. Then being from Louisiana and surviving both Katrina and Rita, every time they interview someone whose home was hit by a hurricane they are going to find the woman in the lime green stretch pants to interview.

Oh wait, for you it might be the guy who always seems to have to go to the bathroom right before the check shows up. You know who I'm talking about, right? Oh if you don't, it might be you.

I love this quote from Dolly Parton. She said "It cost a lot of money to look this cheap."

OK enough of that. That's not the kind of cheap I am talking about. I'm talking about those small business owners who don't think enough of themselves and what they deliver to charge enough for it. I see it time and again and what's worse is that you are cheap and you aren't willing to do anything about it. You aren't willing to charge what you should be charging.

You must Fix Your Pricing

Aren't you tired of being an Under Earning Expert? Aren't you ready to be a highly paid authority in your industry? Did you realize that you get to make that decision? It is not decided by your industry. It is not even decided by your clients. It is your decision and your choice to charge what you are worth.

Why aren't you charging what you are worth? If there is anything I can say every one of my clients have in common it is that they were not charging enough when I met them. They don't think they have enough education to charge more or their clients would never pay more or worse yet their clients are broke. What I know to be true is that you can set your price to anything you want if you understand what your ideal client is looking for and can articulate the value that you have set.

Three Ways Businesses Compete

Throughout history businesses have chosen to compete in one of three areas:

1. **Price**
2. **Value**
3. **Convenience**

I would lay odds that for the majority of you reading this book the answer should not be price. Do you really want to be known as the Wal-Mart or Kmart of your industry? No! You don't want to compete on price. Wouldn't you prefer to be known as the Cadillac of your industry? You want to compete on value like Cadillac or convenience like Amazon.

The problem is that when you let thoughts like "I can't charge that much" determine your pricing you are competing on price.

Let me tell you a story about value and convenience. I don't know about you but I travel a lot which means I end up at the airport a lot. I could park in the regular airport parking lot. My car could sit out in the weather while I am gone and get rained on or other vehicles drive by and get it all dirty and then I could drag my luggage to the bus stop to catch a ride to the terminal and yea I would only have to pay $10 a day for that parking spot. They are competing on price. They believe a parking spot is just a parking spot.

However, I like to park at the Parking Spot and instead of paying $10 a day I pay $19/day. Why would I be willing to pay double for the same old $10 parking spot? Well first my car is going to be covered. It's out of the weather and I like to take care of my car so I definitely want that. Then they are going to drive right up to my car and pick me up. No walking. And there are even times when they take my bags out of my car for me and put them on the shuttle without me touching them. And a couple of hours before I get back my car is going to be hand washed and will be all shiny when I get home. Of course, I paid an extra $14.95 for that car wash before I left. Then they pick me up after my flight, take me to my clean car and put my bags in the trunk for me.

It's still just a place to put my car while I am gone but the value is higher. Then sometimes with higher value comes more opportunity. My car is shiny and clean.

You are nothing but the $10 parking spot because you don't know how to bring value. You don't know how to wash the car at an additional fee.

Now me, I would be a $10 parking spot if I only was a business coach but I figured out my added value and my car wash. I have started and sold multi-million dollar businesses. I have owned retail and service based businesses. I have bought millions of dollars of equipment, employed hundreds of people, spoken in front of very large crowds, hosted my own events and so much more. There is my added value.

"I'm not all things to all people. I'm the best at my thing to the right people – those who want to make money." – Michele Scism

My car wash is the fact that I have spent the time in this business to build a large following and a community of people paying attention so now people are willing to pay me to get in front of my community. I host events and people pay big money to sponsor those events.

You need to understand how to articulate your value in a way that your clients can see it and want to hire you. **Remember that people spend money on what they value. It is your job to show them the value.**

So when you are speaking to your potential new client you aren't going to speak to them about the cost. You are going to talk about the value, the worth. What is it worth to them to get this handled? What is it worth to you to get this business thing handled? Would you spend $10,000 if you knew it was going to bring you $100,000?

The other day I heard that a man spent $10M on a Mastiff. That dog better do more than fetch slippers.

Action Case Study #2

When I met Belanie Dishong in 2010, (LiveAtChoice.com) she had been in business for 17 years. She had a very well developed process for working with her clients. Her clients were seeing amazing results; marriages were saved, families reunited, businesses growing. They loved her, she had a full practice and she loved what she was doing.

But she was broke! Over those 17 years the most she had ever made was $40,000 and that wasn't even enough to cover her expenses. After a few minutes of discussion I knew exactly what the issue was. She wasn't charging enough money. She had people buying a 12 month coaching program with her for $750. Not a month either. That was the cost for the entire program. First we shifted her prices then we did some major work on her internal business systems including a follow up system and created a new re-engagement campaign because she had so many previous clients that could come back for refresher courses. We even added a new delivery method for her coaching so more people could work with her.

In 2013 she had her first $250,000+ year. She faced the fears, made a decision to quite competing on price and took massive action.

Congratulations Belanie!

"What you think about, talk about and get off your ass and do something about is what comes about."

-Larry Winget,
The Pitbull of Personal Responsibility

Entrepreneurs Are Lazy

I didn't say you're not working hard. I said your lazy!

There is a great quote by Jules Renard "Failure is not our only punishment for laziness; there is also the success of others." That quote is a driver for me because as I talked about earlier in the book when you have something on the other side of fear that is big enough and you want bad enough you will do anything. I personally find inspiration, drive and desire in other peoples successes. Part of that may be that I don't want to fail and they succeed but that's my issue, right? LOL

So let's wrap our head around this lazy conversation.

Entrepreneurs are some of the hardest working people I know. You are working hard but you're working hard at doing the stuff you like to do, the things you're good at doing, those things you think are fun instead of doing the stuff that should be done.

You are doing the wrong stuff. You're doing the stuff that doesn't make you one damn dime.

I see it every day. You're working on your website, you're checking your email, you're playing on social media, you're creating another product because that last one didn't sell. When you should be talking to clients, when you should be picking up the phone and having sales conversations, speaking, doing webinars.

My Year as a Lazy Entrepreneur

Let me tell you about my first year in this business. My quick story is that I am a third generation entrepreneur who was born into a family who had children to guarantee they had employees. I started working in the family grocery store at the age of 5. They paid me in toys and I thought I had found my calling. I spent most of my life working in one of our many businesses until after I graduated from college when I started to work exclusively in our trucking company. I told you earlier that we went through some tough times and some good times and the story ended in 2007 when we sold our trucking company and I retired. Then I spent a couple of years trying to reinvent myself. I flipped houses for a while and that was a lot of fun but the credit system put an end to that. For a while I thought I might be a life coach (aren't you glad I realized that wasn't for me?). Then in November of 2009 I ended up in Los Angeles CA at a marketing conference with a business coach on stage. I looked at him and said that's what I want to be. I want to teach people how to build businesses because I am so good at it.

I have to say I really thought I would hang out my shingle and entrepreneurs would start handing me money after all I had just helped build and sell a multi-million dollar company. I know how to build a business! I know how to make money! I am a money magnet! Those were my mantras. But all of a sudden they weren't my reality.

Why was this so hard? Where were all the entrepreneurs who were going to hire me to help them make a lot of money? All of a sudden, I was robbing Peter to pay Paul. I was working from the moment I woke up to the moment I went to bed and then even in bed my brain wouldn't turn off.

You know entrepreneurs are the only people willing to work 80+ hours a week to avoid a 40 hour a week job.

And guess what, I wasn't even making as much as I could have been making working 40 hours a week at McDonalds.

My reality was that I had cash flow but never seemed to have enough money. Constantly in the worry about how I was going to pay that next bill, how I was going to pay my team, how I was going to pay my coach. Are you feeling this?

Remember my mantra: I am a money magnet! The truth is I create lots of cash flow. In 2013 I did half a million in this coaching business but I still wonder sometimes where the money goes and I really hope it sends for me when it gets settled.

One day, after I had been in business for about a year, it was late at night, everyone was asleep and I was sitting at my desk balling, just sobbing uncontrollably and listening to that little Michele in my head. You have no doubt been visited by that voice. She was saying "Just quit!" "You can't do it!" "You've lost all this money." "What makes you think this will work?" "You're so tired." "How long can you keep it up?" "You're doing everything you know how to do."

Then I heard her say "**Well not really!**" And then I started arguing with myself. "What do you mean I'm not doing what I am really supposed to be doing?" "Do you know how hard I work, from the moment I get out of bed till the moment I go to bed?" And she said

"Yea, you're keeping busy to avoid doing what it really takes to build this business."

It was that moment, you know **THE MOMENT**, when we hear something that stops us in our tracks. It was true; I wasn't doing what I knew I had to do to build my business. And here is the really bad news, **YOU AREN'T EITHER!**

- ✓ I wasn't making the phone calls and you aren't either.
- ✓ I wasn't doing the follow up and you aren't either.
- ✓ I wasn't building the relationships and you aren't either.
- ✓ I wasn't putting myself out there and you aren't either.

I was playing to be mediocre. Not playing to win and so are you!

So I made a choice to change all of that. To stop being lazy and start to focus on the things that matter. I started to focus on what I call IPA's (Income Producing Activities). I started to make scary decisions and take actions that brought about big changes in my business.

If I told you that you could pick up a check for $2,200 tomorrow, would you do what was necessary? As I was going through this process of making the right choices and taking the right actions one day my phone rang. It was the director of the Houston eWomen Network chapter and she said "Michele, I've been watching you and I would love for you to come speak at my luncheon. I can't pay you but you could come and talk about your book." Now at that point I had only written my 1st book *"Make Over Your Business in 6 Weeks or Less"* but my business was shifting to be more focused on social media and I wanted to talk about that so I said "Great. Did you hear that I have a new book? It's called *"Take Action Get Profits - 5 Steps to Massive Online Visibility"* She thought that sounded great and booked me to speak two weeks later. I hung up the phone and thought "Well I better write that book." I wrote it in 2 days. I knew I didn't have time to get books printed so I created it as a digital download, an e-book. At the speaking engagement I sold it and a training class and had 22 women hand me $100 each. So I went home with $2200 in my pocket and I was hooked.

Because I was willing to do what it took, I had $2200 that I didn't have the day before. I took the risk. Could it have not worked? Absolutely but I did it anyway. Was I afraid? Absolutely but I did it anyway. Was I being cheap? Yes but I was working on it. Was I lazy? Not at all. I did what it took to create income and put myself out there.

So where are you being lazy?

How many sales calls did you make last week? Are you following up the way you are supposed to? Are you relying on technology to do your business when the thing that really works is person to person meetings, calls and sessions? Now I'm not saying that you don't use online strategies but what I want you to see if that those are relationship building strategies they are not sales strategies. So you can't rely on email to sell your program, you have to pick up the phone.

I can tell you that there is one area of your business that would drastically change everything if you stop being lazy.

Lazy Follow Up Leads to Business Failure

I talk to a lot of entrepreneurs around the country and they all say the same thing "I'm just not good at Follow Up!" You know what, they are right. The statistics are staggering; 80% of all sales are made by 20% of salesmen. That's because they are the ones doing the follow up. They continue to make the phone calls, they mail the birthday cards, they continue to ask for the sale until they get a yes or a go to hell. So let's look at a couple of quick changes you can make to stop your lazy follow up behaviors.

1. Do you have those piles of business cards on your desk that you meant to follow up on? You know you do. And if you don't shame on you, because it probably means you haven't been networking. OK so what you do with all those cards and all the future cards you bring home is to connect with those people on social media. Find them on Facebook, LinkedIn, Twitter, and Pinterest, which ever social media sites are your favorites. Oh here is a little free advice. Never ask to more than 20 people a day to connect with you on Facebook. You could end up with something called the Facebook slap and you don't want it. If you have a VA or a social media person this is a perfect task for them. Once you are connected then schedule a get to know you conversation.

2. How many outbound follow up calls did you make last week? Your second follow up strategy is to do 15 minutes of out bound calls every day. Only 15 minutes. You are going to take that stack of business cards and pull out the ones you really wanted to connect with or your list of previous clients or just those people you have been meaning

to connect with, pickup the 10,000 lb phone and dial. Dial and Smile as we would say in Mary Kay. Oh I don't think I told you I was a Mary Kay Sales Director for 5 years. Your goal from these phone calls is simply to set an appt to talk to them. So if they answer you are going to say something like "Hey Mary, This is Michele Scism. I know you're busy and I only have a few seconds but we met at Suzanne's event and we exchanged cards and said we would connect. I just wanted to set a time for us to talk and get to know each other." You do this for 90 days and you will change your life and your business.

Recently I was in the mall with my husband and I saw the *Coach* Purse store. I love **Coach** Purses and so I looked at my husband and said "You know what, I'm going to pop in this store and you really don't have to come in. If you want I can meet you somewhere." I really was just avoiding the inevitable explosion when he realized that I was looking at $500 purses. But of course, he wanted to come in. I had been looking for my next *Coach* Purse for months and as I walked around the store I spotted it. It was love at first sight. I looked at the tag and it was only $457. The first thought I had was "Great, I'll come back and look at it later when he's not here." I turn around only to hear a little voice say "Would you like to see the different colors we have in that purse?" Well of course I did. Long story short, once I resuscitated my husband, I bought the purse. No, I'm kidding. He played it really cool in the store; I just had to remind him that he had on a pair of $500 Ostrich skin boots at the time.

About a week later I get a card in the mail from the sales girl. Thanking me and wanting to know if I am enjoying my purse. Then she went on to mention that they are going to be getting matching accessories in the store soon that will go

March 15, 2014

Hey Michele,

I had a great time with y'all today! The cafe carryall is a good choice for organization, and the grey is so pretty! We're doing a new flourset soon, so I'm going to email pictures of some of the accessories that will go great! I hope to see you soon!

Thanks so much,
Katie
Prien Lake Coach

great with my purse and she will let me know as soon as they come in so I can come see them. A week later my phone rings and who do you think it was? Yep she just wanted to let me know they got in the new wallet and sunglass case. My new wallet looks fantastic in my new *Coach* Purse.

Of course there are a million other things you can do for follow up but here is what I know. I am not looking for complicated. I am looking for consistent. So I want you to find a few ways that you can follow up. I want you to stay focused on them and I want you to get really good at them. Let them become second nature. Do not over complicate this.

Action Case Study #3

I want to introduce you to Kate Beeders (KateBeeders.com). She is the complete opposite of a lazy entrepreneur. One of those clients we all dream about. A massive action taker who faces her fears and does it anyway and she is committed to consistency.

Kate was presented with a challenge. Make 15 minutes of outbound calls for 90 days. Being one who does not back down from a challenge she completed it. In those 90 days she got new clients, she filled her event, she brought on new sponsors for her event and ended up with multiple joint venture opportunities. Her immediate income in that quarter was $67,000 but that is just a drop in the bucket compared to what those daily actions will produce over the next few years. You see what she has done is create momentum.

Another interesting point is that Kate was one of only three people who actually completed the challenge. The challenge was offered to 150 people but 147 chose not to finish. They chose to quite. Some of them chose to quite before they started and others chose to quite along the way but Kate's commitment to her business is unwavering and thus will lead to massive success. Congratulations Kate!

"Short as life is, we make it still shorter by the careless waste of time."

-Victor Hugo,
French Poet & Novelist

Top 7 Time Suckers for Entrepreneurs

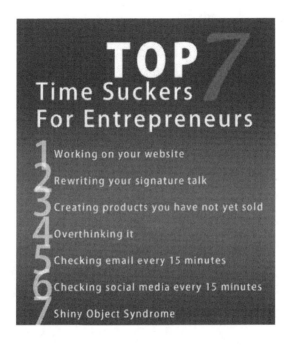

I don't know about you but I love a great top 7 list and in this book I have two for you. We are starting with the top 7 time suckers for entrepreneurs. In case you're not sure, these are the things you should be avoiding on a daily basis. You will probably notice that this looks a lot like a list of things a lazy entrepreneur would focus on. In the next chapter, I will share with you the top 7 daily money making must do's. But I thought we should start with what to avoid, so let's get started.......

1. **Working on your website!** This is a big one. We are never happy with our websites. There are always improvements to be made, things to be added and things we wish we had never put there in the first place. Do not work on your website during the day. Hire someone to do this for you.

2. **Rewriting your signature talk!** So how many times have you modified your talk or reworked your power point? Yes speaking is on the list of must do's but you do not need to recreate the wheel every time you talk.

3. **Creating products you have not yet sold!** This one usually draws fear from those who hear me say it. But I will say it again, if you have not sold it, do not create it. Let me tell you why. I see so many entrepreneurs spending tons of time and money to create products and programs and then their launch falls flat. 99% of the time, they have a good idea but they missed the marketing message. They didn't understand exactly what their audience wants. So now they have created something that won't sell. Instead you can simply create a sales page and get out and sell it. Once people buy it then they become the beta group that you work with to create it. Remember, people will support that which they help create.

4. **Over thinking it!** I can't tell you how often I hear from entrepreneurs who just aren't sure if they are headed in the right direction or what the title of their talk should be or how to choose their next virtual assistant. Over thinking it is a guaranteed way to fail. Of course, you should give some thought to a decision but you have to make a decision, take the risks and if it fails you back up and punt.

5. **Checking email every 15 minutes!** Do I really have to talk about this one? I probably should have started

with this one because it is the biggest time suck you have.

6. **Checking social media every 15 minutes!** Now don't get me wrong. I think social media is an important part of your marketing strategy but if you want to accomplish big things then you have to be careful how much time is wasted on social media. When you are on social media have a plan, stick to it, connect with the people you intended to, interact with a few people, check to make sure you have responded to any important messages and then turn it off.

7. **Shiny Object Syndrome!** You know what this is. You have chosen a direction but then you make the mistake of listening to a few too many free teleclasses and they are saying that if you would only do this it would work better and what you have been doing isn't quite working. Maybe I will just try this for a while you think. Listen success requires consistency. Any plan of action must be followed and implemented to succeed. I get it that sometimes it feels like no one is paying attention or this isn't going to work but the truth is you have to stick to the plan.

So the question is do you go cold turkey or wean yourself off of these? I will leave that one up to you but I would do everything within my power to stop wasting your precious time every day. I'll leave you with these words from Benjamin Franklin, "**Lost time is never found again**."

"Money and Success don't change people;
they merely amplify what is
already there."

-Will Smith,
Actor, Producer, Rapper

Top 7 Daily Money Making to Do's for Entrepreneurs

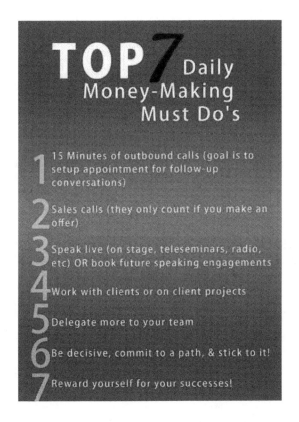

You made it through the tough list. The one that told you what you have to stop doing. Now it is time to start focusing on what you should be doing to make more money in business. These are the income producing activities and actions that will change your business.

1. **15 minutes of outbound calls!** OK we talked about this one already. The goal of these calls is to set up appointments for follow up conversations. They are short and directly to the point. Be ready with your calendar so you can get them scheduled.

2. **Sales calls!** You didn't really think you would only be on the phone for 15 minutes a day did you? You actually have to make the follow up calls that you have now scheduled. The ultimate goal of these calls is to get a new client. Depending on your relationship with this person this may happen on the first call or that first call maybe a getting to know you call which leads into a second conversation to talk about working together. It only counts as a sales call if you make an actual offer of your services and ask for the sale.

3. **Speak or book future speaking engagements!** Remember my $2,200 sales talk at that luncheon? How many of those would you like to do a week? On a daily basis you should spend time either speaking whether that be at a luncheon, on a stage, on a radio show, a teleseminar or webinar, or getting booked for a future speaking engagement. Speaking is one of the fastest ways for you to be seen as an authority in your industry and the fastest way to get people to pay you money even if it is just selling your books in the back of the room.

4. **Work with clients or on client projects!** If you are making the calls and speaking then hopefully you are getting new clients and you have to provide the services you have sold them. Most of the time that implementation is your job. There are times when you can pass that off to your team but it is something you have to focus on daily.

5. **Delegate more to your team!** You might be questioning whether this is an income producing activity or more of a cost center? The fact is when you grow your team and they take over the daily drudgery then you can spend that time on sales calls or working with clients. Your goal should be to give 80% of your to do list away on a daily basis to your team.

6. **Be decisive, commit to a path & stick to it!** We started to talk about this on the last list. It is the opposite of over thinking things or the shiny object syndrome. Being decisive, committed and sticking to it will make you money faster than those people who are constantly changing direction. Do not keep recreating yourself and your business.

7. **Reward yourself for your successes!** This one needs no explanation.

Now you have a plan. Stick to these 7 new habits daily and you will quickly see changes. Brian Tracy says that **"Successful people are just those with successful habits."**

"Some people want it to happen,
some wish it would happen,
others make it happen."

-Michael Jordan,
Professional Basketball Player, Entrepreneur

How Bad Do You Want It?

You hold a dream in your heart and the big question is "Are you will to do what it takes to make that your reality?" That's what this whole book has been about.

You might be asking yourself "Why is this so hard? When is it going to be my turn to get ahead?" It is hard. My husband says "that if it were easy the girl scouts would do it instead of selling cookies that someone else makes for them."

Along this path you are going to have a lot of disappointment, a lot of pain and a lot of doubting yourself. Those things come with the territory but for you these things aren't ends in a tunnel. They are simply hurdles to be cleared.

Success is not reserved for the few; it is available to anyone who is willing to do what it takes to have it. It is your responsibility to go after what you want.

You have to ask yourself one question.

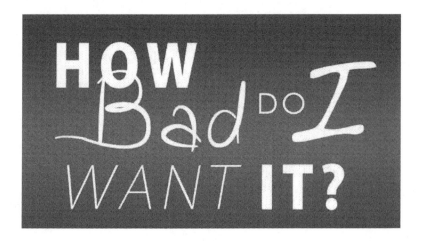

Are you willing to do what it takes to have the business you desire? What are you willing to do? What are you willing to give up? Are you willing to miss the party? Are you willing to go without sleep? Are you willing to be told NO?

It's necessary for you to understand a few things. You are an uncommon breed. Everyone will not see your vision. They will not necessarily join you. They will not understand why this is so important to you. Remember that the only opinion of you that matters is your own. It doesn't matter what others think of you.

"If it is to be, it's up to me." William H Johnsen

Why would you pick up a book titled *"Take The Risks or Get a Job"*? Because you are ready to take responsibility and you are ready for change.

What you need to do is align yourself with the people out there who want more. The people who refuse to leave life just as it is. They are hungry for change and can see the vision when there are no walls and there are no clients and there are no immediate successes on the horizon.

You have to attach yourself to the winners. Mary Kay always said you should "Hold on tight to the tail of a rising star because even if you fall you will land among the stars." Be sure you are following the right people, hire a great coach and secure the best team you can get. These are the people who can help you stay focused on your dreams and stand up against your fears.

"Miracles start to happen when you give as much energy to your dreams as to your fears." Richard Wilkins

It's time for you to stand up and be the person you were designed to be. Step into the success that is rightfully yours. Just get started.

How bad do you want it?

Did you happen to see *Dallas Buyers Club* with Matthew McConaughey? In that movie he lost 35 lbs to play a rodeo cowboy who finds out he is HIV positive and has 30 days to live. Did you see Christian Bale in American Hustle? He gained 50 lbs to play a Bronx swindler. That is a dedication to their craft. How bad do you think they wanted to those roles? You have to be committed to do something like this. How often have you ever said I want to lose weight? Maybe it was your New Year's Resolution. Almost everyone has made that resolution. How many times have you said at the beginning of the year "I want to make more money." The reason you're reading this book is because you want something. That's why you're here. You aren't satisfied with the way it is. There are meetings all over America right now where people are talking about how they want more.

Everybody wants more; the world is full of people who want more. Why don't those people have more? If everyone wants it, why don't they have it? **No commitment.**

Now I have told you what it takes to make this work and I have told you that it takes commitment. None of this matters unless you really want it. There comes a time where information doesn't make a difference unless there is a commitment to the information, a commitment to the action that it is going to take, a commitment to the work. It's a commitment to doing whatever it takes and that's where it falls apart. There is lots of information out there and lots of methods to get what you want but it is still, regardless of which method you choose, your responsibility to take the action and get it done. I don't see a lot of commitment; I see a lot of lip service. I see a lot of people talk about commitment. I see a lot of people talk about making more money.

We started this journey together in this book with the fact that you are broke. You're making money but you're still broke and it's because you're working hard but your working hard on the wrong things.

I told you it's because you are afraid. You're afraid of the changes that it will require to get achieve the success you desire. We talked about fear of spending money, hiring a team, missing your family and taking risks. It simply boils down to the fear of taking risks. How do you over this. You feel the fear and do it anyway. Remember when your desire for what is on the other side is big enough you will do anything to get it.

Then we determined that you are cheap. Not green stretch pants cheap but Wal-Mart and Kmart cheap. You should not be competing on price. Instead focus on value and convenience. Figure out what your car wash is.

And you're lazy. Bill Gates said "I always choose a lazy person to do a difficult job because he will find an easy way to do it." Your kind of lazy is different. It doesn't come from lack of work; it comes from working on the wrong stuff. We talked about learning to focus on income producing activities in your business and avoiding the time sucking things most entrepreneurs do.

That led us directly into two fun top 7 lists. The top 7 time suckers for entrepreneurs and the top 7 money making must do's for entrepreneurs. Be sure you are paying close attention to these lists on a daily basis.

I want you to know that I did all those things too but let me tell you my turning point. In 2013 I hosted a 3 day conference in Houston, Texas. It's called Take Action Get Profits and it is an annual event that I started in 2011. But this particular one was different.

I finally took the right risks, made the right decisions, took the right action and during that 3 day event I stood on that stage and sold $300,000 worth of coaching. You see I had to step into it too.

You have to stop being cheap, stop being lazy and stop being afraid. The instant I stopped being afraid everything changed. I also had to stop being cheap. What you don't know is that the night before that event I was on the phone with my coach begging him to let me drop the price. I didn't believe I could sell a coaching package that was that much money. He said "No! That's your price." The minute I stopped being lazy and started doing the right things I made money. I made more in that 3 day event than most of you have made since you started your businesses.

Remember.....

When you want success as much as you want to breathe then and only then will you find it!
    – Socrates

Additional Inspiration

"In life lots of people know what to do but few people actually do what they know. Knowing is not enough! You must take action."
-Anthony Robbins

"First they ignore you, then they laugh at you, then they fight you, then you win."
-Gandhi

"What lies behind us and what lies before us are tiny matters compared to what lies within us." -Ralph Waldo Emerson

"Chase the vision not the money, the money will end up following you." –Tony Hsieh

"Success is walking from failure to failure with no loss of enthusiasm." –Winston Churchill

Get your **FREE** Companion Video Series

"From Under Earning Expert to Highly Paid Authority"
at

www.HighlyPaidAuthority.com

You will also receive weekly business tips designed specifically for decisive business owners.

You will learn.......

- How to use VIP days to work with clients, add money to your bottom line and have diversity in your offerings.
- How to turn your $10 book or e-book into a $200 product.
- How to increase your conversions and double your sales this year.

If you are ready to start making more money in your business be sure to a quick look at these 3 short videos that are packed with information that you can apply immediately.

So let's get started!

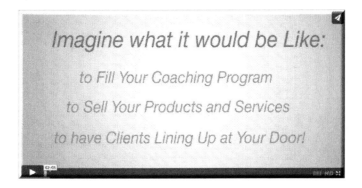

www.HighlyPaid Authority.com

Who is Michele Scism?

Michele Scism is an entrepreneur, wife, mother and advocate for business owners' worldwide. She is best known as The Results Lady and for her amazing speed with which she gained massive visibility for her business, Decisive Minds (www.DecisiveMinds.com).

As a full-time coach, speaker, author, radio show host and trainer Michele partners with small business owners who

have made the decision to take their business to the next level by using her "Take Action Get Profits" formula to attract massive visibility, get more clients and make more money.

She has been featured on several interviews including being interviewed by Kristi Frank of Donald Trump's The Apprentice for her Success Show.

Michele spent most of her life working in family businesses in both the retail and service industries, starting several successful businesses on her own and even spending a few years in the corporate world. She has a degree in Accounting but she has spent her life learning every aspect of business specializing in business strategy and more recently in online visibility.

She is the proud mother of 2 amazing young adults, Allyson and Bryan. She is married to a wonderful man, JE, who is a masterful sales person.

Throughout Michele's life she has been labeled many things, a "self-help" junkie, confident, inspirational, motivational, positive but most importantly mother, wife & daughter. Always interested in self improvement she takes many courses and seminars, lives a positive life and believes that she is responsible for what happens in her life. She is a Christian and believes that through God all things are possible.

Be sure to connect with Michele on your favorite social media channels. Go to www.DecisiveMinds.com for Facebook, Twitter, LinkedIn and YouTube connections.

Fun facts about Michele:

1. She loves drag racing and attends drag races around the country annually.

2. She loves to dance. She competed in country/western dance competitions around the world in the pro-am divisions for many years, holding two national titles.

3. She loves to travel.

4. She collects Santa Clause figurines.

5. She loves learning and quotes.

What Others are Saying About Michele

"I have been working with Michele for over two years and have seen my business go **to 6 figures and beyond**. I accredit most of that to the private planning with Michele. She is a brilliant strategist and can break things down into actionable steps that my team and I can easily implement!"

Belanie Dishong, Founder of Live At Choice

"After working with Michele to create a package deal for my programs I had my **1st ever $25,000 month** and it was in December of all months. I can't wait to see what this next year holds. Thanks Michele!"

Joyce Jagger, Founder of TheEmbroideryCoach.com

"In working with Michele over the last year, she has helped me to devise a strategic plan that has **enabled me create a six-figure income in just my FIRST year of business**. Her teachings are incredibly easy to follow and are time-tested and proven successful. I am so excited to see what my second year of business holds. I couldn't have done it without Michele's experience and guidance!"

Lisa Hendrix, Founder of Serenity Nursing Consultants

Yvonne Phillips

Michele Scism, thank you for the interview on your show today! I got off the call and got a paid client, IMMEDIATELY. Great mojo!!

Unlike · Comment · March 3 at 6:58pm near Pittsburgh, PA

"In just an hour with Michele I got a whole new strategy for my Facebook Fan Page, both in content and in advertising. In just a week, we are **getting as many likes in a day as we got all last month**! And our reach expanded by 10-20x. Plus one tip she gave me is **saving me a ton of time** when posting to my fan page. Michele knows her Facebook, and she keeps up with the trends. I'd highly recommend her!"

Terri Zwierzynski, Founder of Solo-E.com

Kathleen Gage
Online Marketing Strategist and Product Creation Specialist at Power Up for Profits

Michele Scism is one of the most amazing professionals I know. She is visionary, focused and knows how to network in ways that are beyond the norm. I had the opportunity to be a featured expert in Michele's training series and found this to be one of the best experiences I have ever had.

"I can't say enough good things about Michele Scism of Decisive Minds! Michele is the premier expert on Social Media. If you are looking to learn more about how to grow your business using Facebook, LinkedIn, or Twitter, Michele is THE person to ask. Her knowledge regarding how to use these tools far exceeds anyone else in the field. I have attended Michele's seminars and also hired her for one-on-one coaching, and I would recommend her to anyone who is looking to integrate Social Media into their business." *June 25, 2011*

Top qualities: Expert, Good Value, Creative

(1st) Karen Terry, GISP
hired Michele as a Business Consultant in 2011, and hired Michele more than once

Katie Wilber
Thanks for all of the great info from Michele Scism! Loved all the great content and meeting all of you fabulous ladies! Can't wait to connect more with you all!

on Wednesday · Unlike · Comment · Unsubscribe

Peggy Bell Nolan I did a VIP day with Michele Scism - talk about immersion learning and worth every cent. I'm implementing what's always been there but with clarity, purpose, and laser focus. Let's set up a time to chat and catch up! Would love to hear about your conference!

Yesterday at 8:43am via mobile

 Lisa Hendrix

ok, Michele Scism! I listened to our call from last week. I put some of the things you mentioned about taking your freebie and posting it on your "liked" websites into action and I went from 3 people on my new Serenity Nursing Consultants fan page to 58 in less then 24 hours!! AND.....I now have 36 new opt -ins for my new eBook!! I am sooo excited :). You ROCK!

16 minutes ago · Like · Comment · Unsubscribe

👍 Karen Sharp likes this.

 Karen Sharp It worked, Lisa! I just liked it, too!
8 minutes ago · Like

 Lisa Hendrix Thank you!!
6 minutes ago · Like

 Michele Scism WooHoo!! Girl You Rock - you're the one who took the action!
about a minute ago · Like

 Michele, you are an amazing model of giving! What an awesome video full of content and specific tips & strategies for folks to get started on today.

Not only is the content great, this is a terrific "how-to" model-in-action of education-based marketing. Simple watch, learn, and copy! 😊 Thank you!

Tshombe

 Thank you Michele for sharing this great video! I love the way you so clearly and concisely explained how to share your expertise on social media in a very easy to understand format. I learned some new strategies that I plan to implement right away. It was definitely filled with valuable content. I look forward to the next two videos.

Sherry Kane

Lynn Ruby

WHO HOO HOO HOOO HOOOOOO ! I just got back from doing a speech on video marketing for 200 people ! Had a blast! And they loved me! Here are two VERY MAJOR THINGS I learned today:

Good lord, I know more than the majority of business owners out there! Not just about video marketing either. I include websites, wordpress, social media, email marketing and SEO in that basket too. It is astonishing how much our prospective clients don't know. Remember that ladies! They SOOOO need us!

And two - I would NEVER have had this opportunity if Michele Scism hadn't kicked me in the beehind with her velvet boot to get me out there doing a teleseminar on my own which is what lead to today's opportunity! Thank You Michele!

And finally, I came back to the office, did a quick 2 minute video thanking everyone who gave me their business card requesting my free report and got it done and uploaded in about 20 minutes! Modeling imperfect video (which is what I told them in my presentation) to perfection!

And I get to repeat it tomorrow! Thank you thank you thank you all!

Like · Comment · Unfollow Post · 4 hours ago

"Never tell people how to do things. Tell them what to do and they will surprise you with their ingenuity."

General George Patton

You'll get beyond the fear when what's on the other side is important enough.